HEY GOD, I'VE GOT SOME GUY NAMED JONAH IN MY STOMACH AND I THINK I'M GOING TO THROW UP!

THE WHALE TELLS HIS SIDE OF THE STORY

TROY SCHMIDT

ILLUSTRATED BY CORY JONES

HEY. I'M THE WHALE FROM THAT FAMOUS STORY. NO, NOT THE ANGRY WHITE WHALE. AND NO, NOT THE ONE WHO SWALLOWS A PUPPET AND A CRICKET. THE OTHER STORY. ACTUALLY, THE *FIRST* STORY ABOUT A WHALE: THE STORY OF JONAH.

THE TALE HAS BEEN TOLD MILLIONS OF TIMES, BUT PEOPLE ALWAYS TALK ABOUT JONAH AND WHAT *HE* WENT THROUGH. WHAT ABOUT ME? I HAD SOME GUY STUCK IN MY STOMACH! AND HE DIDN'T TASTE VERY GOOD EITHER. LET ME TELL YOU MY SIDE OF THE STORY.

ONE DAY I WAS SWIMMING AROUND, EATING MY USUAL FOUR THOUSAND POUNDS OF FISH FOR THE DAY, WHEN GOD SPOKE TO ME. "WHALE," HE SAID. "I HAVE A JOB FOR YOU TO DO. I WANT YOU TO SWALLOW A HUMAN."

I COULDN'T BELIEVE MY TINY EARS. "A HUMAN? BUT THEY LIVE ON LAND." LAND CREATURES TASTE LIKE DIRT. YEEECCCH. GOD REPLIED, "YOU HAVE TO TRUST ME."

"I CAN'T DO IT," I SAID.
AND THEN I REALIZED I HAD JUST TOLD GOD NO. MY ONLY
THOUGHT WAS TO GET OUT OF THERE, PRONTO. SO I SWAM
AS FAST AS I COULD. I SWAM AS FAR AWAY AS I COULD. I
THOUGHT I WOULD BE SAFE ONCE I GOT OUT OF THERE.
AT LEAST, I THOUGHT . . . UNTIL—

GAAGGGKK!

SOMETHING GOT STUCK IN MY THROAT. WHAT WAS THIS? IT WASN'T A DOLPHIN. MUCH BIGGER. IT WASN'T A SHARK. I HAD SWALLOWED ONE OF THOSE BEFORE. TALK ABOUT A SORE THROAT! NOPE, THIS WAS LARGER AND IT MOVED AROUND A LOT, KICKING AND SCREAMING AND YELLING. AND THE TASTE! I'VE EATEN BLOWFISH AND SEAWEED, BUT THIS WAS AWFUL. IT TASTED . . . IT TASTED LIKE . . . DIRT. OH NO.

"OH MY," THE DOCTOR CRIED.

"WHAT IS IT?"

"OH MY," THE DOCTOR SIGHED.

"WHAT IS IT!"

"OH MY," THE DOCTOR REPLIED.

"YOU SWALLOWED SOME GUY.

HE'S IN YOUR STOMACH."

I HAD SEEN THE HUMANS BEFORE. THEY SAILED ON THEIR GREAT SHIPS WHICH SCARED ME, MAINLY BECAUSE THEY WERE BAD DRIVERS. ONE BOAT BUMPED INTO ME, AND THEY DIDN'T EVEN STOP TO APOLOGIZE. MOST FISH WILL AT LEAST STOP AND SAY THEY'RE SORRY FOR THE LITTLE "FIN"-DER BENDER. NOT THE HUMANS. THEY THINK THEY OWN THIS PLANET.

"CAN YOU GET HIM OUT?" I ASKED DR. CRAB, FEELING A LITTLE QUEASY.

"NOTHING I CAN DO. YOU JUST HAVE TO WAIT A DAY. IT'LL PASS."

I DIDN'T LIKE THE SOUND OF THAT.

THAT WHOLE DAY, I COULDN'T SWIM VERY FAR. I COULDN'T TALK VERY MUCH. AND GET THIS: I COULDN'T EAT A BITE. NOW FOR ME, THAT'S A BIG DEAL. HOW WOULD YOU LIKE IT IF YOU HAD SOMETHING IN YOUR STOMACH TOSSING AND TURNING AND KICKING THE WALLS OF YOUR TUMMY?

AND THE YELLING! I COULDN'T SLEEP BECAUSE OF ALL THE YELLING.
"GOD, IT'S ME, JONAH!" (THAT'S HOW I FOUND OUT HIS NAME.) "GET ME
OUT OF HERE! IT STINKS IN HERE!" HEY, IT WASN'T EASY FOR ME EITHER,
BUT YOU DIDN'T HEAR ME COMPLAINING! OKAY, MAYBE JUST A LITTLE.

BUT I ALSO HEARD JONAH DO SOMETHING ELSE. PRAY. AT LEAST HE BELIEVED IN GOD. NOW ALL ANIMALS, AND I SPEAK FOR THE SEA CREATURES, BELIEVE IN GOD. IT'S OBVIOUS HE CREATED ALL OF US. SO I WAS GLAD TO KNOW THAT THIS HUMAN BELIEVED IN GOD TOO. AND I THOUGHT JONAH PROBABLY HAD THE RIGHT IDEA. SO I PRAYED.

"LORD," I SAID, "I DIDN'T
LISTEN TO YOU. I RAN AWAY FROM
WHAT YOU WANTED ME TO DO. I'M SORRY."
"THAT'S OKAY, WHALE. IT WILL ALL
WORK OUT," GOD SAID.
"GREAT. SO CAN YOU GET THIS STINKY,
SMELLY HUMAN BEING OUT OF ME?"
"I'M SORRY, WHALE. I CAN'T DO
THAT YET," GOD REPLIED.
"WHY NOT?" I CRIED.
"YOU HAVE TO TRUST ME."
AND THAT WAS ALL GOD SAID.

THE SECOND DAY WAS NOT MUCH BETTER. JONAH SLOWED DOWN HIS KICKING, WHICH WAS NICE. I THINK HE WAS GETTING TIRED. WORD GOT OUT TO THE SEA CREATURES ABOUT THIS HUMAN BEING INSIDE MY STOMACH. EVERYONE WANTED TO SEE. EVEN SCHOOLS OF FISH TOOK FIELD TRIPS TO SEE THE MAN IN MY STOMACH.

AND THE OTHER WHALES TEASED ME.
"YOU DON'T LOOK SO GOOD.
SOMETHING YOU ATE?" THEY LAUGHED.
"STEP BACK GUYS! HE'S GONNA BLOW!"
LOTS MORE LAUGHTER.
BELIEVE ME, I WANTED THIS GUY OUT, BUT
I ALSO REMEMBERED WHAT GOD SAID.
"YOU HAVE TO TRUST ME."

THE THIRD DAY WAS THE WORST.
ALL NIGHT I COULDN'T SLEEP. ALL DAY I
COULDN'T THINK. INSIDE, JONAH MOVED VERY LITTLE.
I STARTED TO THINK HE WAS, YOU KNOW . . . ASLEEP.
I PRAYED AGAIN TO GOD. "WHY DID YOU PUT THIS GUY
IN MY STOMACH? FOR THREE DAYS I'VE BEEN SICK."
GOD ANSWERED BACK VERY QUIETLY. "WHALE, I
NEEDED YOU TO HOLD HIM UNTIL HE WAS READY
TO FOLLOW ME. YOU SEE, HE TRIED TO RUN AWAY
WHEN I ASKED HIM TO DO SOMETHING."
"SOUNDS FAMILIAR," I SAID, ASHAMED THAT I HAD
RUN AWAY FROM GOD TOO.
"FOR THREE DAYS HE WAS LEARNING TO TRUST ME,
JUST AS YOU WERE. WHEN HE GETS OUT, HE WILL TELL
A MESSAGE TO THOUSANDS OF PEOPLE WHO WILL
FOLLOW ME. AND YOU ARE PART OF
THAT PLAN."

"ME?"

"YOU ARE GOING TO BECOME ONE OF THE MOST
FAMOUS WHALES IN HISTORY BECAUSE OF WHAT YOU DID.
AND ALL YOU HAD TO DO WAS TRUST ME."
I COULDN'T BELIEVE IT. I WAS ACTUALLY A PART OF GOD'S PLAN.
ME, AN ORDINARY FIVE-TON WHALE, HELPING GOD BRING A
MESSAGE OF HOPE TO PEOPLE ALL OVER THE WORLD.
SUDDENLY MY STOMACHACHE WASN'T SO BAD. SUDDENLY MY
HEART FELT A LITTLE GLAD. ALL I HAD TO DO WAS TRUST GOD.
"NOW, WHALE, IT IS TIME. GET THIS MAN TO LAND AS
FAST AS YOU CAN!"

I SPED PAST DR. CRAB WHO TRIED TO HELP.
I FLEW PAST THE SCHOOLS OF FISH THAT WERE CURIOUS TO SEE.
I BLEW BY THE WHALES WHO LAUGHED AT ME.
I COULDN'T STOP. I HAD A JOB TO DO FOR GOD.

ALL OF A SUDDEN MY STOMACH REALLY STARTED TO HURT. IT TWISTED, TURNED, GURGLED, GAGGED, THEN—BLLLLAAAAAGHHHHHHH! JONAH CAME FLYING OUT OF MY STOMACH ALONG WITH EVERYTHING ELSE I HAD EATEN THAT WEEK. IT WAS DISGUSTING.

I HAVE TO ADMIT MY AIM WAS PRETTY GOOD.

HE LANDED RIGHT ON THE BEACH.

JONAH PICKED HIMSELF UP, AND I SAW HIM FOR THE FIRST TIME.

HE BRUSHED HIMSELF OFF AND TURNED TO ME. "THANK YOU, WHALE.

SORRY I MADE YOU FEEL SO BAD. I LEARNED A LOT IN THE PAST THREE DAYS."

SO DID I, I THOUGHT.

I LATER HEARD THAT JONAH OBEYED GOD AND DID GREAT THINGS.

MANY PEOPLE CAME TO KNOW GOD AND PUT THEIR FAITH IN HIM.

AND I HELPED, BECAUSE I TRUSTED GOD.

FROM THEN ON, I DID
WHATEVER GOD ASKED . . .
AND WATCHED WHAT I ATE.
THE
END.